macaroons

macaroons

30 recipes for perfect bite-sized treats

First published in 2011
LOVE FOOD is an imprint of Parragon Books Ltd

Parragon
Queen Street House
4 Queen Street
Bath BA1 1HE, UK

ISBN: 978-1-4454-3448-3

Printed in China
All photography by Clive Streeter, except front cover (© Cindy Loughridge/Getty Images)

Recipes and home economy by Angela Drake

Notes for the Reader
This book uses both metric and imperial measurements. Follow the same units of measurement throughout; do not mix metric and imperial. All spoon measurements are level: teaspoons are assumed to be 5 ml, and tablespoons are assumed to be 15 ml. Unless otherwise stated, milk is assumed to be full fat, eggs and individual vegetables are medium, and pepper is freshly ground black pepper.

The times given are an approximate guide only. Preparation times differ according to the techniques used by different people and the cooking times may also vary from those given. Optional ingredients, variations or serving suggestions have not been included in the calculations.

Recipes using raw or very lightly cooked eggs should be avoided by infants, the elderly, pregnant women, convalescents and anyone suffering from an illness. Pregnant and breastfeeding women are advised to avoid eating peanuts and peanut products. Sufferers from nut allergies should be aware that some of the ready-made ingredients used in the recipes in this book may contain nuts. Always check the packaging before use.

Contents

Introduction   6

Classic Flavours   12

Fancy Flavours   28

Fruity Flavours   46

Something Special   64

Index   80

Introduction

French *macarons* or macaroons are small almond meringues sandwiched together with a flavoured filling to make delightful bite-sized sweet treats. Made from egg whites, ground almonds, and caster and icing sugars, they are characterized by their smooth domed tops, frilly edged bases and wonderfully soft and slightly chewy centres. Popular in French patisseries, where a dazzling array of colours and flavours can be found, macaroons are the perfect after-dinner treat, sweet gift, teatime fancy or wedding favour.

As simple as they look, macaroons can be a little tricky to make – indeed pastry chefs can spend years perfecting the art of macaroons. But don't let that put you off because this book has everything you need to know for successful macaroon making – from a guide to the essential equipment and ingredients you will need, to clear and detailed step-by-step instructions for the basic method used to make all the macaroons in the book.

Once you've mastered the basic technique, you can try any one of the 30 deliciously different macaroons in this book. From classic flavours, such as vanilla, chocolate and pistachio, to more unusual combinations, such as sesame and lime or even peanut butter and jam, you'll be spoilt for choice.

So what are you waiting for? You may not quite achieve the high standards of a French pastry chef with your first few batches, but follow the top tips on the opposite and following pages and you'll soon find that the art of making macaroons is a pleasurable pastime with the most fabulous results!

- If your piping skills are not too good, mark circles on the baking paper by dipping a small cutter or the end of a large piping nozzle into icing sugar and tapping it onto the paper. It's not a problem if the circles vary in size – just match up the macaroons according to size when pairing them together.

- Use the oven temperature stated in the recipes as a guide – once you have made a couple of batches of macaroons you may find that the temperature of your oven needs reducing or increasing a little to achieve the best results. Use an oven thermometer if you have one. Fan ovens cook more quickly than conventional ovens so reduce the temperature by 10–20°C/50–68°F. You may also find that they cook the macaroons a little quicker – usually in about 9–10 minutes. On the other hand, gas ovens produce a more uneven, moist heat so try leaving the oven door slightly ajar to allow any steam to escape and rotate the sheet after 5–6 minutes.

- If you find that the bases of the macaroons are browning too quickly, place the baking sheet on a second baking sheet to diffuse the heat. If the tops of the macaroons crack, the oven temperature is too high.

- If the macaroon shells stick to the baking paper, try spraying a little water between the paper and baking sheet to create a little steam, which will help to release them.

- Unfilled macaroons will keep for 3–4 days in an airtight container or freeze for up to 1 month. Filled macaroons will keep in the fridge for 2–3 days, depending on the type of filling. They are best eaten at room temperature a few hours after filling.

10 Steps to Macaroon Perfection

Refer to this simple step-by-step guide when making any of the macaroon recipes in the book.

STEP 1: Place the ground almonds and icing sugar in a food processor and process for about 15 seconds, until the mixture is fine and powdery. Sift the mixture into a bowl through a large sieve. Discard any fine bits of almond left in the sieve.

STEP 2: Whisk the egg whites until holding soft peaks. Gradually whisk in the caster sugar, about 1 tablespoon at a time. Whisk well after each addition to make a firm and glossy meringue. The meringue should look like shaving cream and hold stiff peaks when the whisk is lifted from the bowl.

STEP 3: Add one third of the almond mixture to the meringue. Using a spatula, fold the dry mixture into the meringue. Use a circular folding action by running the spatula around the bowl and under the meringue then folding and cutting through the mixture.

STEP 4: Once all the dry mixture has been folded into the meringue, add the second third of the almond mixture, repeating the folding and cutting action. As more dry ingredients are folded into the meringue it will become firmer.

STEP 5: Add the final third of the almond mixture and repeat the folding and cutting action. Once all the dry ingredients have been incorporated the mixture will be quite firm so continue mixing until the consistency of the mixture loosens. The final batter should be smooth and glossy and a thick ribbon of batter should fall slowly from the spatula, leaving a trail for about 30 seconds before disappearing.

Important: Under-mixing the macaroon mixture will result in a batter that is too firm and the piped macaroons will have peaks. Over-mixing will result in a runny batter that will not hold its shape when piped. Check the batter every few turns of the spatula to avoid over-mixing.

STEP 6: Line two baking sheets with baking paper. Pour the mixture into a large piping bag fitted with a 1-cm/½-inch nozzle. Pipe 3-cm/1¼-inch rounds onto the prepared baking sheets. Make sure the rounds are well spaced. For large macaroons pipe 7-cm/2¾-inch rounds and for mini macaroons pipe 2-cm/¾-inch rounds.

STEP 7: Tap the underside of the baking sheets firmly with the palm of your hand or tap onto a work surface to remove any air bubbles and settle any small peaks and bumps. This action also helps the frilly foot (or *pied*) to form during baking. Any peaks still remaining can be flattened by dabbing gently with a wetted fingertip.

STEP 8: Leave the macaroons to stand at room temperature for 30 minutes to allow the surface of each macaroon to dry and form a slight crust. You should be able to gently touch the surface without any mixture sticking to your finger.

STEP 9: Bake the macaroons, one baking sheet at a time. Check after 5–6 minutes – if they are overbrowning, reduce the oven temperature slightly. Cooking time will take 10–15 minutes, depending on your oven, so check again after 10 minutes. The macaroons are ready when they have a crisp shell and the frilly foot at the base does not wobble when the shells are gently lifted from the paper. If the bases are still soft and sticky, return the trays to the oven for a further few minutes, leaving the door ajar.

STEP 10: Leave the macaroons to cool on the baking sheets for 10 minutes. Carefully peel them away from the paper. Leave to cool completely on a wire rack.

Essential Equipment

Scales
Accurate measuring is one of the major keys to success when making macaroons. Always follow the same units of measurement – do not mix metric and imperial.

Food processor
To achieve a really finely ground almond and icing sugar mixture you will need a food processor with a sharp blade. A large blender will work just as well. A coffee or spice grinder will also be useful for finely grinding nuts and seeds to flavour the macaroons.

Sieve
To remove any pieces of almond from the processed mixture, a large sieve with medium–fine holes is essential. Sifting the mixture also helps to remove any lumps that may have formed during processing.

Electric whisk
A hand-held electric whisk makes light work of whisking egg whites and making meringue. Choose one with at least three speed settings.

Spatula
Folding the ground almonds and icing sugar into the meringue mixture is the most vital stage of macaroon making and for this you will need a firm-handled rubber or silicone spatula with a flexible tip.

Baking sheets
It's worth investing in a couple of solid baking sheets that won't buckle in the oven to ensure neatly shaped macaroons. Line with non-stick baking paper.

Piping bag and nozzle
For piping perfect macaroons onto the baking sheet make sure you have a large-capacity piping bag. Nylon, fabric or sturdy disposable bags can be used. A plastic or metal plain nozzle with a 1-cm/½-inch hole is also needed.

Basic Ingredients

It only takes a few basic ingredients to make simple macaroon shells.

Ground almonds
These give macaroons their slightly chewy texture and nutty flavour. Although they are available to buy ready-ground in the supermarket, they need to be processed to a finer texture before using to give a smooth finish to the baked macaroons.

Icing sugar
The ground almonds are processed with icing sugar to create a super-fine dry mixture that is easy to fold into the meringue.

Egg whites
In common with any kind of baking, eggs should be used at room temperature when making macaroons. If you have time, separate the eggs a few hours before making the macaroons and leave the whites in a bowl covered loosely with kitchen paper. This allows some moisture to evaporate from the whites.

Food colourings
These can be either in paste or liquid form. A small amount of paste will give a good strong colour so add sparingly. If using liquid colouring, whisk it into the meringue a few drops at a time. Adding colouring will create more moisture in the batter so you may find that brightly coloured macaroons will take a few more minutes to cook.

Flavourings
All kinds of flavourings can be used in macaroons, from ground nuts and seeds to citrus rind, spices, coffee and tea. Add dry flavourings, such as spices, to the almond and icing sugar mixture, and liquid or moist flavourings, such as vanilla extract or lemon rind, to the meringue mixture.

Classic Flavours

Vanilla Macaroons

makes 16

75 g/2¾ oz ground almonds

115 g/4 oz icing sugar

2 large egg whites

50 g/1¾ oz caster sugar

½ tsp vanilla extract

filling

55 g/2 oz unsalted butter, softened

½ tsp vanilla extract

115 g/4 oz icing sugar, sifted

Place the ground almonds and icing sugar in a food processor and process for 15 seconds. Sift the mixture into a bowl. Line two baking sheets with baking paper.

Place the egg whites in a large bowl and whisk until holding soft peaks. Gradually whisk in the caster sugar to make a firm, glossy meringue. Whisk in the vanilla extract.

Using a spatula, fold the almond mixture into the meringue one third at a time. When all the dry ingredients are thoroughly incorporated, continue to cut and fold the mixture until it forms a shiny batter with a thick, ribbon-like consistency.

Pour the mixture into a piping bag fitted with a 1-cm/½-inch plain nozzle. Pipe 32 small rounds onto the prepared baking sheets. Tap the baking sheets firmly onto a work surface to remove air bubbles. Leave at room temperature for 30 minutes. Preheat the oven to 160°C/325°F/Gas Mark 3.

Bake in the preheated oven for 10–15 minutes. Cool for 10 minutes, then carefully peel the macaroons off the baking paper. Leave to cool completely.

To make the filling, beat the butter and vanilla extract in a bowl until pale and fluffy. Gradually beat in the icing sugar until smooth and creamy. Use to sandwich pairs of macaroons together.

Chocolate Macaroons

makes 16

75 g/2¾ oz ground almonds

100 g/3½ oz icing sugar

2 tbsp cocoa powder

2 large egg whites

50 g/1¾ oz caster sugar

filling

100 g/3½ oz good-quality plain chocolate, finely chopped

150 ml/5 fl oz double cream

Place the ground almonds, icing sugar and cocoa powder in a food processor and process for 15 seconds. Sift the mixture into a bowl. Line two baking sheets with baking paper.

Place the egg whites in a large bowl and whisk until holding soft peaks. Gradually whisk in the caster sugar to make a firm, glossy meringue.

Using a spatula, fold the almond mixture into the meringue one third at a time. When all the dry ingredients are thoroughly incorporated, continue to cut and fold the mixture until it forms a shiny batter with a thick, ribbon-like consistency.

Pour the mixture into a piping bag fitted with a 1-cm/½-inch plain nozzle. Pipe 32 small rounds onto the prepared baking sheets. Tap the baking sheets firmly onto a work surface to remove air bubbles. Leave at room temperature for 30 minutes. Preheat the oven to 160°C/325°F/Gas Mark 3.

Bake in the preheated oven for 10–15 minutes. Cool for 10 minutes, then carefully peel the macaroons off the baking paper. Leave to cool completely.

To make the filling, place the chocolate in a heatproof bowl. Heat the cream in a saucepan until just boiling, then pour over the chocolate and stir until smooth. Leave to cool for 15–20 minutes, stirring occasionally, until thickened. Use to sandwich pairs of macaroons together.

Rosewater Macaroons

makes 16

75 g/2¾ oz ground almonds

115 g/4 oz icing sugar

2 large egg whites

50 g/1¾ oz caster sugar

½ tsp rosewater

pink food colouring paste or liquid

1 tbsp small crystallized rose petals

filling

150 ml/5 fl oz double cream

2 tsp rosewater

Place the ground almonds and icing sugar in a food processor and process for 15 seconds. Sift the mixture into a bowl. Line two baking sheets with baking paper.

Place the egg whites in a large bowl and whisk until holding soft peaks. Gradually whisk in the caster sugar to make a firm, glossy meringue. Whisk in the rosewater and enough food colouring to give a pale pink colour.

Using a spatula, fold the almond mixture into the meringue one third at a time. When all the dry ingredients are thoroughly incorporated, continue to cut and fold the mixture until it forms a shiny batter with a thick, ribbon-like consistency.

Pour the mixture into a piping bag fitted with a 1-cm/½-inch plain nozzle. Pipe 32 small rounds onto the prepared baking sheets. Tap the baking sheets firmly onto a work surface to remove air bubbles. Top half the macaroons with 2–3 crystallized rose petals. Leave at room temperature for 30 minutes. Preheat the oven to 160°C/325°F/Gas Mark 3.

Bake in the preheated oven for 10–15 minutes. Cool for 10 minutes, then carefully peel the macaroons off the baking paper. Leave to cool completely.

To make the filling, whisk the cream and rosewater together until holding soft peaks. Use to sandwich pairs of macaroons together.

Pistachio Macaroons

makes 16

50 g/1¾ oz ground almonds

25 g/1 oz pistachio nuts,
finely ground, plus 2 tbsp
finely chopped to decorate

115 g/4 oz icing sugar

2 large egg whites

50 g/1¾ oz caster sugar

green food colouring
paste or liquid

filling

55 g/2 oz unsalted butter,
softened

green food colouring
paste or liquid

115 g/4 oz icing sugar, sifted

2 tbsp pistachio nuts,
finely chopped

Place the ground almonds, ground pistachio nuts and icing sugar in a food processor and process for 15 seconds. Sift the mixture into a bowl. Line two baking sheets with baking paper.

Place the egg whites in a large bowl and whisk until holding soft peaks. Gradually whisk in the caster sugar to make a firm, glossy meringue. Whisk in enough food colouring to give a pale green colour.

Using a spatula, fold the almond mixture into the meringue one third at a time. When all the dry ingredients are thoroughly incorporated, continue to cut and fold the mixture until it forms a shiny batter with a thick, ribbon-like consistency.

Pour the mixture into a piping bag fitted with a 1-cm/½-inch plain nozzle. Pipe 32 small rounds onto the prepared baking sheets. Tap the baking sheets firmly onto a work surface to remove air bubbles. Sprinkle over the chopped pistachios. Leave at room temperature for 30 minutes. Preheat the oven to 160°C/325°F/Gas Mark 3.

Bake in the preheated oven for 10–15 minutes. Cool for 10 minutes, then carefully peel the macaroons off the baking paper. Leave to cool completely.

To make the filling, beat the butter and a little food colouring in a bowl. Gradually beat in the icing sugar until smooth and creamy. Stir in the pistachio nuts. Use to sandwich pairs of macaroons together.

Coffee Cream Macaroons

makes 16

75 g/2¾ oz ground almonds

1 tsp coffee granules, finely crushed

115 g/4 oz icing sugar

2 large egg whites

50 g/1¾ oz caster sugar

1 tbsp coffee sugar crystals, lightly crushed

filling

55 g/2 oz full-fat soft cheese

25 g/1 oz unsalted butter, softened

2 tsp cold strong black coffee

115 g/4 oz icing sugar, sifted

Place the ground almonds, coffee granules and icing sugar in a food processor and process for 15 seconds. Sift the mixture into a bowl. Line two baking sheets with baking paper.

Place the egg whites in a large bowl and whisk until holding soft peaks. Gradually whisk in the caster sugar to make a firm, glossy meringue.

Using a spatula, fold the almond mixture into the meringue one third at a time. When all the dry ingredients are thoroughly incorporated, continue to cut and fold the mixture until it forms a shiny batter with a thick, ribbon-like consistency.

Pour the mixture into a piping bag fitted with a 1-cm/½-inch plain nozzle. Pipe 32 small rounds onto the prepared baking sheets. Tap the baking sheets firmly onto a work surface to remove air bubbles. Sprinkle over the sugar crystals. Leave at room temperature for 30 minutes. Preheat the oven to 160°C/325°F/Gas Mark 3.

Bake in the preheated oven for 10–15 minutes. Cool for 10 minutes, then carefully peel the macaroons off the baking paper. Leave to cool completely.

To make the filling, place all the ingredients in a bowl and, using an electric whisk, beat until smooth. Use to sandwich pairs of macaroons together.

Lemon Macaroons

makes 16

75 g/2¾ oz ground almonds
115 g/4 oz icing sugar
2 large egg whites
50 g/1¾ oz caster sugar
finely grated rind of ½ lemon
yellow food colouring
paste or liquid

filling
115 g/4 oz mascarpone
cheese
finely grated rind of ½ lemon
1 tsp lemon juice
4 tbsp lemon curd

Place the ground almonds and icing sugar in a food processor and process for 15 seconds. Sift the mixture into a bowl. Line two baking sheets with baking paper.

Place the egg whites in a large bowl and whisk until holding soft peaks. Gradually whisk in the caster sugar to make a firm, glossy meringue. Whisk in the lemon rind and enough food colouring to give a bright yellow colour.

Using a spatula, fold the almond mixture into the meringue one third at a time. When all the dry ingredients are thoroughly incorporated, continue to cut and fold the mixture until it forms a shiny batter with a thick, ribbon-like consistency.

Pour the mixture into a piping bag fitted with a 1-cm/½-inch plain nozzle. Pipe 32 small rounds onto the prepared baking sheets. Tap the baking sheets firmly onto a work surface to remove air bubbles. Leave at room temperature for 30 minutes. Preheat the oven to 160°C/325°F/Gas Mark 3.

Bake in the preheated oven for 10–15 minutes. Cool for 10 minutes, then carefully peel the macaroons off the baking paper. Leave to cool completely.

To make the filling, beat the mascarpone and lemon rind and juice together until smooth. Spread the lemon curd over half the macaroons and the mascarpone mixture over the other half. Carefully sandwich together in pairs.

Hazelnut Chocolate Macaroons

makes 16

50 g/1¾ oz ground almonds

25 g/1 oz hazelnuts, finely ground, plus 1 tbsp chopped to decorate

115 g/4 oz icing sugar

2 large egg whites

50 g/1¾ oz caster sugar

6 tbsp hazelnut and chocolate spread

Place the ground almonds, ground hazelnuts and icing sugar in a food processor and process for 15 seconds. Sift the mixture into a bowl. Line two baking sheets with baking paper.

Place the egg whites in a large bowl and whisk until holding soft peaks. Gradually whisk in the caster sugar to make a firm, glossy meringue.

Using a spatula, fold the almond mixture into the meringue one third at a time. When all the dry ingredients are thoroughly incorporated, continue to cut and fold the mixture until it forms a shiny batter with a thick, ribbon-like consistency.

Pour the mixture into a piping bag fitted with a 1-cm/½-inch plain nozzle. Pipe 32 small rounds onto the prepared baking sheets. Tap the baking sheets firmly onto a work surface to remove air bubbles. Sprinkle over the chopped hazelnuts. Leave at room temperature for 30 minutes. Preheat the oven to 160°C/325°F/Gas Mark 3.

Bake in the preheated oven for 10–15 minutes. Cool for 10 minutes, then carefully peel the macaroons off the baking paper. Leave to cool completely.

Sandwich pairs of macaroons together with the hazelnut and chocolate spread.

Fancy Flavours

Saffron & Cardamom Macaroons

makes 16

75 g/2¾ oz ground almonds

115 g/4 oz icing sugar

2 large egg whites

¼ tsp saffron strands, crushed, plus extra strands to decorate

50 g/1¾ oz caster sugar

yellow food colouring paste or liquid

filling

55 g/2 oz unsalted butter, softened

seeds from 4 cardamom pods, finely crushed

115 g/4 oz icing sugar, sifted

Place the ground almonds and icing sugar in a food processor and process for 15 seconds. Sift the mixture into a bowl. Line two baking sheets with baking paper.

Place the egg whites and crushed saffron strands in a large bowl and whisk until holding soft peaks. Gradually whisk in the caster sugar to make a firm, glossy meringue. Whisk in enough food colouring to give a pale yellow colour.

Using a spatula, fold the almond mixture into the meringue one third at a time. When all the dry ingredients are thoroughly incorporated, continue to cut and fold the mixture until it forms a shiny batter with a thick, ribbon-like consistency.

Pour the mixture into a piping bag fitted with a 1-cm/½-inch plain nozzle. Pipe 32 small rounds onto the prepared baking sheets. Tap the baking sheets firmly onto a work surface to remove air bubbles. Sprinkle over the extra saffron strands. Leave at room temperature for 30 minutes. Preheat the oven to 160°C/325°F/Gas Mark 3.

Bake in the preheated oven for 10–15 minutes. Cool for 10 minutes, then carefully peel the macaroons off the baking paper. Leave to cool completely.

To make the filling, beat the butter and cardamom seeds in a bowl until pale and fluffy. Gradually beat in the icing sugar until smooth and creamy. Use to sandwich pairs of macaroons together.

Chocolate Ginger Macaroons

makes 16

75 g/2¾ oz ground almonds
115 g/4 oz icing sugar
1 tsp ground ginger
2 large egg whites
50 g/1¾ oz caster sugar

filling
25 g/1 oz unsalted butter
1 tbsp stem ginger syrup
85 g/3 oz plain chocolate, broken into pieces
4 tbsp double cream
1 piece stem ginger, finely chopped

Place the ground almonds, icing sugar and ground ginger in a food processor and process for 15 seconds. Sift the mixture into a bowl. Line two baking sheets with baking paper.

Place the egg whites in a large bowl and whisk until holding soft peaks. Gradually whisk in the caster sugar to make a firm, glossy meringue.

Using a spatula, fold the almond mixture into the meringue one third at a time. When all the dry ingredients are thoroughly incorporated, continue to cut and fold the mixture until it forms a shiny batter with a thick, ribbon-like consistency.

Pour the mixture into a piping bag fitted with a 1-cm/½-inch plain nozzle. Pipe 32 small rounds onto the prepared baking sheets. Tap the baking sheets firmly onto a work surface to remove air bubbles. Leave at room temperature for 30 minutes. Preheat the oven to 160°C/325°F/Gas Mark 3.

Bake in the preheated oven for 10–15 minutes. Cool for 10 minutes, then carefully peel the macaroons off the baking paper. Leave to cool completely.

To make the filling, melt the butter, ginger syrup and chocolate in a heatproof bowl set over a pan of simmering water. Remove from the heat and stir in the cream and stem ginger. Cool for 20 minutes, stirring occasionally. Use to sandwich pairs of macaroons together.

Peanut Butter & Jam Macaroons

makes 16

50 g/1¾ oz ground almonds
25 g/1 oz natural roasted peanuts, finely ground
115 g/4 oz icing sugar
2 large egg whites
50 g/1¾ oz caster sugar
1 tbsp salted peanuts, finely chopped

filling
4 tbsp peanut butter
2 tbsp seedless raspberry jam

Place the ground almonds, ground roasted peanuts and icing sugar in a food processor and process for 15 seconds. Sift the mixture into a bowl. Line two baking sheets with baking paper.

Place the egg whites in a large bowl and whisk until holding soft peaks. Gradually whisk in the caster sugar to make a firm, glossy meringue.

Using a spatula, fold the almond mixture into the meringue one third at a time. When all the dry ingredients are thoroughly incorporated, continue to cut and fold the mixture until it forms a shiny batter with a thick, ribbon-like consistency.

Pour the mixture into a piping bag fitted with a 1-cm/½-inch plain nozzle. Pipe 32 small rounds onto the prepared baking sheets. Tap the baking sheets firmly onto a work surface to remove air bubbles. Sprinkle over the chopped salted peanuts. Leave at room temperature for 30 minutes. Preheat the oven to 160°C/325°F/ Gas Mark 3.

Bake in the preheated oven for 10–15 minutes. Cool for 10 minutes, then carefully peel the macaroons off the baking paper. Leave to cool completely.

Sandwich pairs of macaroons together with the peanut butter and jam.

Green Tea Macaroons

makes 16

75 g/2¾ oz ground almonds

115 g/4 oz icing sugar,
plus extra for dusting

2 tsp green tea leaves

2 large egg whites

50 g/1¾ oz caster sugar

green food colouring
paste or liquid

filling

55 g/2 oz unsalted butter,
softened

juice and finely grated
rind of ½ lemon

115 g/4 oz icing sugar, sifted

Place the ground almonds, icing sugar and green tea in a food processor and process for 15 seconds. Sift the mixture into a bowl. Line two baking sheets with baking paper.

Place the egg whites in a large bowl and whisk until holding soft peaks. Gradually whisk in the caster sugar to make a firm, glossy meringue. Whisk in enough green food colouring to give a pale green colour.

Using a spatula, fold the almond mixture into the meringue one third at a time. When all the dry ingredients are thoroughly incorporated, continue to cut and fold the mixture until it forms a shiny batter with a thick, ribbon-like consistency.

Pour the mixture into a piping bag fitted with a 1-cm/½-inch plain nozzle. Pipe 32 small rounds onto the prepared baking sheets. Tap the baking sheets firmly onto a work surface to remove air bubbles. Leave at room temperature for 30 minutes. Preheat the oven to 160°C/325°F/Gas Mark 3.

Bake in the preheated oven for 10–15 minutes. Cool for 10 minutes, then carefully peel the macaroons off the baking paper. Leave to cool completely.

To make the filling, beat the butter and lemon juice and rind in a bowl until pale and fluffy. Gradually beat in the icing sugar until smooth and creamy. Use to sandwich pairs of macaroons together. Dust with icing sugar.

Sesame & Lime Macaroons

makes 16

50 g/1¾ oz ground almonds

3 tbsp toasted sesame seeds, finely ground, plus 1 tsp extra to decorate

115 g/4 oz icing sugar

2 large egg whites

50 g/1¾ oz caster sugar

filling

115 g/4 oz medium-fat soft cheese

juice and finely grated rind of ½ lime

2 tbsp icing sugar, sifted

green food colouring paste or liquid

Place the ground almonds, ground sesame seeds and icing sugar in a food processor and process for 15 seconds. Sift the mixture into a bowl. Line two baking sheets with baking paper.

Place the egg whites in a large bowl and whisk until holding soft peaks. Gradually whisk in the caster sugar to make a firm, glossy meringue.

Using a spatula, fold the almond mixture into the meringue one third at a time. When all the dry ingredients are thoroughly incorporated, continue to cut and fold the mixture until it forms a shiny batter with a thick, ribbon-like consistency.

Pour the mixture into a piping bag fitted with a 1-cm/½-inch plain nozzle. Pipe 32 small rounds onto the prepared baking sheets. Tap the baking sheets firmly onto a work surface to remove air bubbles. Sprinkle over the sesame seeds. Leave at room temperature for 30 minutes. Preheat the oven to 160°C/325°F/Gas Mark 3.

Bake in the preheated oven for 10–15 minutes. Cool for 10 minutes, then carefully peel the macaroons off the baking paper. Leave to cool completely.

To make the filling, beat the soft cheese, lime juice and rind and icing sugar until smooth. Add enough food colouring to give a pale green colour. Use to sandwich pairs of macaroons together.

Mint Chocolate Macaroons

makes 16

75 g/2¾ oz ground almonds
115 g/4 oz icing sugar
2 large egg whites
50 g/1¾ oz caster sugar
1 tsp peppermint extract
green food colouring paste or liquid
2 tbsp chocolate sprinkles

filling
55 g/2 oz unsalted butter, softened
55 g/2 oz icing sugar
55 g/2 oz milk chocolate, melted and cooled for 15 minutes

Place the ground almonds and icing sugar in a food processor and process for 15 seconds. Sift the mixture into a bowl. Line two baking sheets with baking paper.

Place the egg whites in a large bowl and whisk until holding soft peaks. Gradually whisk in the caster sugar to make a firm, glossy meringue. Whisk in the peppermint extract and enough green food colouring to give a bright green colour.

Using a spatula, fold the almond mixture into the meringue one third at a time. When all the dry ingredients are thoroughly incorporated, continue to cut and fold the mixture until it forms a shiny batter with a thick, ribbon-like consistency.

Pour the mixture into a piping bag fitted with a 1-cm/½-inch plain nozzle. Pipe 32 small rounds onto the prepared baking sheets. Tap the baking sheets firmly onto a work surface to remove air bubbles. Top with the chocolate sprinkles. Leave at room temperature for 30 minutes. Preheat the oven to 160°C/325°F/Gas Mark 3.

Bake in the preheated oven for 10–15 minutes. Cool for 10 minutes, then carefully peel the macaroons off the baking paper. Leave to cool completely.

To make the filling, beat the butter until pale and fluffy. Sift in the icing sugar and beat thoroughly until smooth and creamy, then fold in the melted chocolate. Use to sandwich pairs of macaroons together.

Violet & Lavender Macaroons

makes 16

75 g/2¾ oz ground almonds

115 g/4 oz icing sugar

2 large egg whites

50 g/1¾ oz lavender sugar

violet food colouring paste or liquid

1 tsp crystallized violets

1 tsp dried lavender

filling

115 g/4 oz soft cheese

2 tbsp lavender sugar

Place the ground almonds and icing sugar in a food processor and process for 15 seconds. Sift the mixture into a bowl. Line two baking sheets with baking paper.

Place the egg whites in a large bowl and whisk until holding soft peaks. Gradually whisk in the lavender sugar to make a firm, glossy meringue. Whisk in enough food colouring to give a pale violet colour.

Using a spatula, fold the almond mixture into the meringue one third at a time. When all the dry ingredients are thoroughly incorporated, continue to cut and fold the mixture until it forms a shiny batter with a thick, ribbon-like consistency.

Pour the mixture into a piping bag fitted with a 1-cm/½-inch plain nozzle. Pipe 32 small rounds onto the prepared baking sheets. Tap the baking sheets firmly onto a work surface to remove air bubbles. Sprinkle over the crystallized violets and dried lavender. Leave at room temperature for 30 minutes. Preheat the oven to 160°C/325°F/Gas Mark 3.

Bake in the preheated oven for 10–15 minutes. Cool for 10 minutes, then carefully peel the macaroons off the baking paper. Leave to cool completely.

To make the filling, beat together the soft cheese and lavender sugar until smooth. Use to sandwich pairs of macaroons together.

Tiramisù Macaroons

makes 16

75 g/2¾ oz ground almonds

1 tsp coffee granules, finely crushed

115 g/4 oz icing sugar

2 large egg whites

50 g/1¾ oz caster sugar

1 tsp cocoa powder

filling

115 g/4 oz mascarpone cheese

1 tbsp marsala or sweet sherry

25 g/1 oz caster sugar

2 tbsp grated milk or plain chocolate

Place the ground almonds, coffee granules and icing sugar in a food processor and process for 15 seconds. Sift the mixture into a bowl. Line two baking sheets with baking paper.

Place the egg whites in a large bowl and whisk until holding soft peaks. Gradually whisk in the caster sugar to make a firm, glossy meringue.

Using a spatula, fold the almond mixture into the meringue one third at a time. When all the dry ingredients are thoroughly incorporated, continue to cut and fold the mixture until it forms a shiny batter with a thick, ribbon-like consistency.

Pour the mixture into a piping bag fitted with a 1-cm/½-inch plain nozzle. Pipe 32 small rounds onto the prepared baking sheets. Tap the baking sheets firmly onto a work surface to remove air bubbles. Sift the cocoa powder over the macaroons. Leave at room temperature for 30 minutes. Preheat the oven to 160°C/325°F/ Gas Mark 3.

Bake in the preheated oven for 10–15 minutes. Cool for 10 minutes, then carefully peel the macaroons off the baking paper. Leave to cool completely.

To make the filling, beat the mascarpone, marsala and caster sugar together until smooth. Spread the mascarpone mixture over half the macaroons, sprinkle over the grated chocolate and top with the remaining macaroons.

Fruity Flavours

Strawberry Macaroons

makes 16

75 g/2¾ oz ground almonds

115 g/4 oz icing sugar, plus extra for dusting

2 large egg whites

50 g/1¾ oz caster sugar

pink food colouring paste or liquid

filling

55 g/2 oz unsalted butter, softened

½ tsp vanilla extract

115 g/4 oz icing sugar, sifted

4 strawberries, hulled and finely chopped

Place the ground almonds and icing sugar in a food processor and process for 15 seconds. Sift the mixture into a bowl. Line two baking sheets with baking paper.

Place the egg whites in a large bowl and whisk until holding soft peaks. Gradually whisk in the caster sugar to make a firm, glossy meringue. Whisk in enough food colouring to give a bright pink colour.

Using a spatula, fold the almond mixture into the meringue one third at a time. When all the dry ingredients are thoroughly incorporated, continue to cut and fold the mixture until it forms a shiny batter with a thick, ribbon-like consistency.

Pour the mixture into a piping bag fitted with a 1-cm/½-inch plain nozzle. Pipe 32 small rounds onto the prepared baking sheets. Tap the baking sheets firmly onto a work surface to remove air bubbles. Leave at room temperature for 30 minutes. Preheat the oven to 160°C/325°F/Gas Mark 3.

Bake in the preheated oven for 10–15 minutes. Cool for 10 minutes, then carefully peel the macaroons off the baking paper. Leave to cool completely.

To make the filling, beat the butter and vanilla extract in a bowl until pale and fluffy. Gradually beat in the icing sugar until smooth and creamy. Fold in the strawberries. Use to sandwich pairs of macaroons together. Dust with icing sugar.

Tangy Orange Macaroons

makes 16

75 g/2¾ oz ground almonds
115 g/4 oz icing sugar
2 large egg whites
50 g/1¾ oz caster sugar
2 tsp finely grated orange rind
orange food colouring paste or liquid
4 tbsp orange marmalade

Place the ground almonds and icing sugar in a food processor and process for 15 seconds. Sift the mixture into a bowl. Line two baking sheets with baking paper.

Place the egg whites in a large bowl and whisk until holding soft peaks. Gradually whisk in the caster sugar to make a firm, glossy meringue. Whisk in the orange rind and enough food colouring to give a bright orange colour.

Using a spatula, fold the almond mixture into the meringue one third at a time. When all the dry ingredients are thoroughly incorporated, continue to cut and fold the mixture until it forms a shiny batter with a thick, ribbon-like consistency.

Pour the mixture into a piping bag fitted with a 1-cm/½-inch plain nozzle. Pipe 32 small rounds onto the prepared baking sheets. Tap the baking sheets firmly onto a work surface to remove air bubbles. Leave at room temperature for 30 minutes. Preheat the oven to 160°C/325°F/Gas Mark 3.

Bake in the preheated oven for 10–15 minutes. Cool for 10 minutes, then carefully peel the macaroons off the baking paper. Leave to cool completely.

Sandwich pairs of macaroons together with the marmalade.

Spiced Apple Macaroons

makes 16

75 g/2¾ oz ground almonds

115 g/4 oz icing sugar

1 tsp ground cinnamon

2 large egg whites

50 g/1¾ oz caster sugar

½ tsp freshly grated nutmeg

filling

450 g/1 lb cooking apples, peeled, cored and chopped

3 tbsp caster sugar

1 tbsp water

Place the ground almonds, icing sugar and cinnamon in a food processor and process for 15 seconds. Sift the mixture into a bowl. Line two baking sheets with baking paper.

Place the egg whites in a large bowl and whisk until holding soft peaks. Gradually whisk in the caster sugar to make a firm, glossy meringue.

Using a spatula, fold the almond mixture into the meringue one third at a time. When all the dry ingredients are thoroughly incorporated, continue to cut and fold the mixture until it forms a shiny batter with a thick, ribbon-like consistency.

Pour the mixture into a piping bag fitted with a 1-cm/½-inch plain nozzle. Pipe 32 small rounds onto the prepared baking sheets. Tap the baking sheets firmly onto a work surface to remove air bubbles. Sprinkle over the grated nutmeg. Leave at room temperature for 30 minutes. Preheat the oven to 160°C/325°F/Gas Mark 3.

Bake in the preheated oven for 10–15 minutes. Cool for 10 minutes, then carefully peel the macaroons off the baking paper. Leave to cool completely.

To make the filling, place the apples, sugar and water in a small pan. Cover and simmer for 10 minutes, until soft. Mash with a fork to make a purée, then leave to cool. Use to sandwich pairs of macaroons together.

Nutty Banana & Toffee Macaroons

makes 16

50 g/1¾ oz ground almonds

25 g/1 oz pecan nuts, finely ground, plus 1 tbsp chopped to decorate

115 g/4 oz icing sugar

2 large egg whites

50 g/1¾ oz caster sugar

filling

½ small banana, finely chopped

4 tbsp dulce de leche (toffee sauce)

Place the ground almonds, ground pecan nuts and icing sugar in a food processor and process for 15 seconds. Sift the mixture into a bowl. Line two baking sheets with baking paper.

Place the egg whites in a large bowl and whisk until holding soft peaks. Gradually whisk in the caster sugar until you have a firm, glossy meringue.

Using a spatula, fold the almond mixture into the meringue one third at a time. When all the dry ingredients are thoroughly incorporated, continue to cut and fold the mixture until it forms a shiny batter with a thick, ribbon-like consistency.

Pour the mixture into a piping bag fitted with a 1-cm/½-inch plain nozzle. Pipe 32 small rounds onto the prepared baking sheets. Tap the baking sheets firmly onto a work surface to remove air bubbles. Sprinkle over the chopped pecan nuts. Leave at room temperature for 30 minutes. Preheat the oven to 160°C/325°F/Gas Mark 3.

Bake in the preheated oven for 10–15 minutes. Cool for 10 minutes, then carefully peel the macaroons off the baking paper. Leave to cool completely.

To make the filling, mix together the banana and dulce de leche. Use to sandwich pairs of macaroons together.

Mango & Passion Fruit Macaroons

makes 16

75 g/2¾ oz ground almonds
115 g/4 oz icing sugar
2 large egg whites
50 g/1¾ oz caster sugar
½ tsp vanilla extract
yellow food colouring paste or liquid
1 piece ready-to-eat dried mango, finely chopped

filling

150 ml/5 fl oz double cream
3 tbsp mango purée
2 tbsp passion fruit pulp

Place the ground almonds and icing sugar in a food processor and process for 15 seconds. Sift the mixture into a bowl. Line two baking sheets with baking paper.

Place the egg whites in a large bowl and whisk until holding soft peaks. Gradually whisk in the caster sugar to make a firm, glossy meringue. Whisk in the vanilla extract and enough food colouring to give a bright yellow colour.

Using a spatula, fold the almond mixture into the meringue one third at a time. When all the dry ingredients are thoroughly incorporated, continue to cut and fold the mixture until it forms a shiny batter with a thick, ribbon-like consistency.

Pour the mixture into a piping bag fitted with a 1-cm/½-inch plain nozzle. Pipe 32 small rounds onto the prepared baking sheets. Tap the baking sheets firmly onto a work surface to remove air bubbles. Top with the dried mango. Leave at room temperature for 30 minutes. Preheat the oven to 160°C/325°F/Gas Mark 3.

Bake in the preheated oven for 10–15 minutes. Cool for 10 minutes, then carefully peel the macaroons off the baking paper. Leave to cool completely.

To make the filling, whip the cream until holding soft peaks, then fold in the mango purée and passion fruit pulp. Use to sandwich pairs of macaroons together.

Blueberry Cheesecake Macaroons

makes 16

75 g/2¾ oz ground almonds
115 g/4 oz icing sugar
2 large egg whites
50 g/1¾ oz caster sugar
½ tsp vanilla extract
blue food colouring paste or liquid

filling
115 g/4 oz soft cheese
2 tbsp soured cream
1 tbsp icing sugar
85 g/3 oz fresh blueberries, lightly crushed

Place the ground almonds and icing sugar in a food processor and process for 15 seconds. Sift the mixture into a bowl. Line two baking sheets with baking paper.

Place the egg whites in a large bowl and whisk until holding soft peaks. Gradually whisk in the caster sugar to make a firm, glossy meringue. Whisk in the vanilla extract and enough food colour to give a bright blue colour.

Using a spatula, fold the almond mixture into the meringue one third at a time. When all the dry ingredients are thoroughly incorporated, continue to cut and fold the mixture until it forms a shiny batter with a thick, ribbon-like consistency.

Pour the mixture into a piping bag fitted with a 1-cm/½-inch plain nozzle. Pipe 32 small rounds onto the prepared baking sheets. Tap the baking sheets firmly onto a work surface to remove air bubbles. Leave at room temperature for 30 minutes. Preheat the oven to 160°C/325°F/Gas Mark 3.

Bake in the preheated oven for 10–15 minutes. Cool for 10 minutes, then carefully peel the macaroons off the baking paper. Leave to cool completely.

To make the filling, beat the soft cheese, soured cream and icing sugar together until smooth. Fold in the crushed blueberries. Use to sandwich pairs of macaroons together.

Raspberry Ripple Macaroons

makes 16

75 g/2¾ oz ground almonds
115 g/4 oz icing sugar
2 large egg whites
50 g/1¾ oz caster sugar
pink food colouring
paste or liquid

filling
150 ml/5 fl oz double cream
1 tsp vanilla extract
3 tbsp raspberry jam

Place the ground almonds and icing sugar in a food processor and process for 15 seconds. Sift the mixture into a bowl. Line two baking sheets with baking paper.

Place the egg whites in a large bowl and whisk until holding soft peaks. Gradually whisk in the caster sugar to make a firm, glossy meringue. Whisk in enough food colouring to give a bright pink colour.

Using a spatula, fold the almond mixture into the meringue one third at a time. When all the dry ingredients are thoroughly incorporated, continue to cut and fold the mixture until it forms a shiny batter with a thick, ribbon-like consistency.

Pour the mixture into a piping bag fitted with a 1-cm/½-inch plain nozzle. Pipe 32 small rounds onto the prepared baking sheets. Tap the baking sheets firmly onto a work surface to remove air bubbles. Use the tip of a cocktail stick to swirl a little food colouring through the top of each macaroon. Leave at room temperature for 30 minutes. Preheat the oven to 160°C/325°F/Gas Mark 3.

Bake in the preheated oven for 10–15 minutes. Cool for 10 minutes, then carefully peel the macaroons off the baking paper. Leave to cool completely.

To make the filling, whip the cream and vanilla extract together until holding soft peaks. Sandwich pairs of macaroons together with the vanilla cream and jam.

Coconut & Pineapple Macaroons

makes 16

50 g/1¾ oz ground almonds

25 g/1 oz desiccated coconut, finely ground, plus 2 tbsp toasted to decorate

115 g/4 oz icing sugar

2 large egg whites

50 g/1¾ oz caster sugar

filling

55 g/2 oz unsalted butter

2 tsp pineapple juice

115 g/4 oz icing sugar, sifted

2 canned pineapple rings, drained and finely chopped

Place the ground almonds, ground coconut and icing sugar in a food processor and process for 15 seconds. Sift the mixture into a bowl. Line two baking sheets with baking paper.

Place the egg whites in a large bowl and whisk until holding soft peaks. Gradually whisk in the caster sugar until you have a firm, glossy meringue.

Using a spatula, fold the almond mixture into the meringue one third at a time. When all the dry ingredients are thoroughly incorporated, continue to cut and fold the mixture until it forms a shiny batter with a thick, ribbon-like consistency.

Pour the mixture into a piping bag fitted with a 1-cm/½-inch plain nozzle. Pipe 32 small rounds onto the prepared baking sheets. Tap the baking sheets firmly onto a work surface to remove air bubbles. Sprinkle over the toasted coconut. Leave at room temperature for 30 minutes. Preheat the oven to 160°C/325°F/Gas Mark 3.

Bake in the preheated oven for 10–15 minutes. Cool for 10 minutes, then carefully peel the macaroons off the baking paper. Leave to cool completely.

To make the filling, beat the butter and pineapple juice in a bowl until pale and fluffy. Gradually beat in the icing sugar until smooth and creamy, then fold in the chopped pineapple. Use to sandwich pairs of macaroons together.

Something Special

Sweetheart Macaroons

makes 6

75 g/2¾ oz ground almonds

115 g/4 oz icing sugar

2 large egg whites

50 g/1¾ oz caster sugar

pink food colouring paste or liquid

filling

115 g/4 oz white chocolate, finely chopped

300 ml/10 fl oz double cream

Place the ground almonds and icing sugar in a food processor and process for 15 seconds. Sift the mixture into a bowl. Line two baking sheets with baking paper and, using a 7-cm/2¾-inch heart-shaped cutter, mark 12 heart shapes on the underside of the paper.

Place the egg whites in a large bowl and whisk until holding soft peaks. Gradually whisk in the caster sugar to make a firm, glossy meringue. Whisk in enough food colouring to give a pink colour.

Using a spatula, fold the almond mixture into the meringue one third at a time. When all the dry ingredients are thoroughly incorporated, continue to cut and fold the mixture until it forms a shiny batter with a thick, ribbon-like consistency.

Pour the mixture into a piping bag fitted with a 1-cm/½-inch plain nozzle. Pipe heart shapes onto the prepared baking sheets. Tap the baking sheets firmly onto a work surface to remove air bubbles. Leave at room temperature for 30 minutes. Preheat the oven to 160°C/325°F/Gas Mark 3.

Bake in the preheated oven for 15–20 minutes. Cool for 10 minutes, then carefully peel the macaroons off the baking paper. Leave to cool completely.

To make the filling, place the chocolate in a heatproof bowl. Heat half the cream in a saucepan until boiling, then pour over the chocolate and stir until smooth. Leave until cold. Whip the remaining cream until holding soft peaks and fold into the chocolate mixture. Use to sandwich pairs of macaroons together.

Summer Berry Macaroons

makes 6

75 g/2¾ oz ground almonds
115 g/4 oz icing sugar
2 large egg whites
50 g/1¾ oz caster sugar
fresh mint sprigs, to decorate

filling

150 ml/5 fl oz double cream
2 tbsp lemon curd
115 g/4 oz small strawberries, hulled and quartered, plus extra whole strawberries to decorate
115 g/4 oz raspberries
2 tbsp icing sugar

Place the ground almonds and icing sugar in a food processor and process for 15 seconds. Sift the mixture into a bowl. Line two baking sheets with baking paper.

Place the egg whites in a large bowl and whisk until holding soft peaks. Gradually whisk in the caster sugar to make a firm, glossy meringue.

Using a spatula, fold the almond mixture into the meringue one third at a time. When all the dry ingredients are thoroughly incorporated, continue to cut and fold the mixture until it forms a shiny batter with a thick, ribbon-like consistency.

Pour the mixture into a piping bag fitted with a 1-cm/½-inch plain nozzle. Pipe 12 large rounds onto the prepared baking sheets. Tap the baking sheets firmly onto a work surface to remove air bubbles. Leave at room temperature for 30 minutes. Preheat the oven to 160°C/325°F/Gas Mark 3.

Bake in the preheated oven for 15–20 minutes. Cool for 10 minutes, then carefully peel the macaroons off the baking paper. Leave to cool completely.

To make the filling, whip the cream until holding soft peaks, then fold in the lemon curd. Top half the macaroon shells with the lemon cream and two thirds of the berries. Purée the remaining berries with the icing sugar. Drizzle the purée over the berries and top with the remaining macaroons. Serve decorated with mint sprigs and whole strawberries.

Mont Blanc Macaroons

makes 6

75 g/2¾ oz ground almonds

100 g/3½ oz icing sugar, plus extra for dusting

2 tbsp cocoa powder

2 large egg whites

50 g/1¾ oz caster sugar

filling

200 ml/7 fl oz double cream

4 tbsp sweetened chestnut purée

2 tbsp plain chocolate shavings

Place the ground almonds, icing sugar and cocoa powder in a food processor and process for 15 seconds. Sift the mixture into a bowl. Line two baking sheets with baking paper.

Place the egg whites in a large bowl and whisk until holding soft peaks. Gradually whisk in the caster sugar to make a firm, glossy meringue.

Using a spatula, fold the almond mixture into the meringue one third at a time. When all the dry ingredients are thoroughly incorporated, continue to cut and fold the mixture until it forms a shiny batter with a thick, ribbon-like consistency.

Pour the mixture into a piping bag fitted with a 1-cm/½-inch plain nozzle. Pipe 12 large rounds onto the prepared baking sheets. Tap the baking sheets firmly onto a work surface to remove air bubbles. Leave at room temperature for 30 minutes. Preheat the oven to 160°C/325°F/Gas Mark 3.

Bake in the preheated oven for 15–20 minutes. Cool for 10 minutes and then carefully peel the macaroons off the baking paper. Leave to cool completely.

To make the filling, whip the cream until holding soft peaks and fold into the chestnut purée. Pipe the chestnut mixture onto half the macaroons. Top with chocolate shavings and the remaining macaroon shells. Serve dusted with icing sugar.

Christmas Macaroons

makes 16

75 g/2¾ oz ground almonds

115 g/4 oz icing sugar

1 tsp ground mixed spice

2 large egg whites

50 g/1¾ oz golden caster sugar

½ tsp freshly grated nutmeg

1 tsp gold dragées

filling

55 g/2 oz unsalted butter, softened

juice and finely grated rind of ½ orange

1 tsp ground mixed spice

115 g/4 oz icing sugar, sifted

25 g/1 oz glacé cherries, finely chopped

Place the ground almonds, icing sugar and mixed spice in a food processor and process for 15 seconds. Sift the mixture into a bowl. Line two baking sheets with baking paper.

Place the egg whites in a large bowl and whisk until holding soft peaks. Gradually whisk in the caster sugar to make a firm, glossy meringue.

Using a spatula, fold the almond mixture into the meringue one third at a time. When all the dry ingredients are thoroughly incorporated, continue to cut and fold the mixture until it forms a shiny batter with a thick, ribbon-like consistency.

Pour the mixture into a piping bag fitted with a 1-cm/½-inch plain nozzle. Pipe 32 small rounds onto the prepared baking sheets. Tap the baking sheets firmly onto a work surface to remove air bubbles. Sprinkle half the macaroons with the grated nutmeg and gold dragées. Leave at room temperature for 30 minutes. Preheat the oven to 160°C/325°F/Gas Mark 3.

Bake in the preheated oven for 10–15 minutes. Cool for 10 minutes, then carefully peel the macaroons off the baking paper. Leave to cool completely.

To make the filling, beat the butter and orange juice and rind in a bowl until fluffy. Gradually beat in the mixed spice and icing sugar until smooth and creamy. Fold in the glacé cherries. Use to sandwich pairs of macaroons together.

Rum Truffle Macaroons

makes 16

75 g/2¾ oz ground almonds

115 g/4 oz icing sugar,
plus extra for dusting

2 large egg whites

50 g/1¾ oz caster sugar

½ tsp vanilla extract

cocoa powder, for dusting

filling

115 g/4 oz plain chocolate,
broken into pieces

25 g/1 oz unsalted butter

75 ml/2½ fl oz double cream

1 tbsp rum

Place the ground almonds and icing sugar in a food processor and process for 15 seconds. Sift the mixture into a bowl. Line two baking sheets with baking paper.

Place the egg whites in a large bowl and whisk until holding soft peaks. Gradually whisk in the caster sugar to make a firm, glossy meringue. Whisk in the vanilla extract.

Using a spatula, fold the almond mixture into the meringue one third at a time. When all the dry ingredients are thoroughly incorporated, continue to cut and fold the mixture until it forms a shiny batter with a thick, ribbon-like consistency.

Pour the mixture into a piping bag fitted with a 1-cm/½ -inch plain nozzle. Pipe 32 small rounds onto the prepared baking sheets. Tap the baking sheets firmly onto a work surface to remove air bubbles. Leave at room temperature for 30 minutes. Preheat the oven to 160°C/325°F/Gas Mark 3.

Bake in the preheated oven for 10–15 minutes. Cool for 10 minutes, then carefully peel the macaroons off the baking paper. Leave to cool completely.

To make the filling, melt the chocolate and butter in a heatproof bowl set over a pan of simmering water. Remove from the heat and stir in the cream and rum. Cool for 10 minutes, then chill in the refrigerator for 30–40 minutes, until thick enough to spread. Use to sandwich pairs of macaroons together. Dust one half of each macaroon with icing sugar and the other half with cocoa powder.

Mini Macaroons

makes 30

75 g/2¾ oz ground almonds
115 g/4 oz icing sugar
2 large egg whites
50 g/1¾ oz caster sugar
½ tsp vanilla extract
selection of sugar sprinkles, to decorate

filling

85g/3 oz unsalted butter, softened
1 tsp vanilla extract
175 g/6 oz icing sugar, sifted
pink, yellow and green food colouring pastes or liquids

Place the ground almonds and icing sugar in a food processor and process for 15 seconds. Sift the mixture into a bowl. Line two baking sheets with baking paper.

Place the egg whites in a large bowl and whisk until holding soft peaks. Gradually whisk in the caster sugar to make a firm, glossy meringue. Whisk in the vanilla extract.

Using a spatula, fold the almond mixture into the meringue one third at a time. When all the dry ingredients are thoroughly incorporated, continue to cut and fold the mixture until it forms a shiny batter with a thick, ribbon-like consistency.

Pour the mixture into a piping bag fitted with a 1-cm/½ -inch plain nozzle. Pipe 60 tiny rounds onto the prepared baking sheets. Tap the baking sheets firmly onto a work surface to remove air bubbles. Top with the sprinkles. Leave at room temperature for 30 minutes. Preheat the oven to 160°C/325°F/Gas Mark 3.

Bake in the preheated oven for 10–14 minutes. Cool for 10 minutes, then carefully peel the macaroons off the baking paper. Leave to cool completely.

To make the filling, beat the butter and vanilla extract in a bowl until pale and fluffy. Gradually beat in the icing sugar until smooth and creamy. Divide the buttercream into three bowls and colour each with pink, yellow or green food colouring. Use to sandwich pairs of macaroons together.

Chocolate Macaroon Gateau

serves 14

85 g/3 oz plain chocolate, broken into pieces

175 g/6 oz unsalted butter, softened, plus extra for greasing

175 g/6 oz caster sugar

175 g/6 oz self-raising flour

½ tsp baking powder

3 large eggs, beaten

2 tbsp cocoa powder

14 chocolate macaroon shells (see page 16)

white and plain chocolate curls, to decorate

icing and filling

175 g/6 oz plain chocolate, finely chopped

450 ml/16 fl oz double cream

Preheat the oven to 180°C/350°F/Gas Mark 4. Grease two 23-cm/ 9-inch sandwich tins and line the bases with baking paper. Melt the chocolate in a heatproof bowl set over a pan of simmering water. Remove from the heat and cool, stirring occasionally.

Place the butter, sugar, flour, baking powder, eggs and cocoa powder in a large bowl and, using an electric whisk, beat until smooth and creamy. Fold in the melted chocolate.

Spoon the mixture into the prepared tins and level the surfaces. Bake in the preheated oven for 20–25 minutes, or until risen and just firm to the touch. Leave to cool in the tins for 5 minutes, then turn out and leave to cool completely.

For the icing, place the chocolate in a heatproof bowl. Heat 300 ml/ 10 fl oz of the cream in a saucepan until just boiling, then pour over the chocolate and stir until smooth. Leave to cool for 20–30 minutes, stirring occasionally, until thick enough to spread. Whip the remaining cream until holding soft peaks.

Sandwich the cakes together with one third of the chocolate icing and all the whipped cream. Spread the remaining icing over the top and sides of the cake. Gently press the macaroon shells onto the icing around the side of the cake. Decorate the top with chocolate curls.

apples: Spiced Apple Macaroons 52

bananas: Nutty Banana & Toffee
  Macaroons 54
Blueberry Cheesecake
  Macaroons 58

cardamom: Saffron & Cardamom
  Macaroons 30
cherries, glacé: Christmas
  Macaroons 72
chestnut purée: Mont Blanc
  Macaroons 70
chocolate
  Chocolate Ginger Macaroons 32
  Chocolate Macaroon Gateau 78
  Chocolate Macaroons 16
  Hazelnut Chocolate Macaroons 26
  Mint Chocolate Macaroons 40
  Mont Blanc Macaroons 70
  Rum Truffle Macaroons 74
  Sweetheart Macaroons 65
  Tiramisù Macaroons 44
Christmas Macaroons 72
Coconut & Pineapple Macaroons 62
coffee
  Coffee Cream Macaroons 22
  Tiramisù Macaroons 44
cream
  Chocolate Ginger Macaroons 32
  Chocolate Macaroon Gateau 78
  Chocolate Macaroons 16
  Mango & Passion Fruit
    Macaroons 56
  Mont Blanc Macaroons 70
  Raspberry Ripple Macaroons 60
  Rosewater Macaroons 18
  Rum Truffle Macaroons 74
  Summer Berry Macaroons 68
  Sweetheart Macaroons 65
  see also soured cream

dulce de leche: Nutty Banana &
  Toffee Macaroons 54

egg whites 11

flavourings 11
food colourings 11

fruit
  Blueberry Cheesecake
    Macaroons 58
  Coconut & Pineapple
    Macaroons 62
  Lemon Macaroons 24
  Mango & Passion Fruit
    Macaroons 56
  Nutty Banana & Toffee
    Macaroons 54
  Raspberry Ripple Macaroons 60
  Spiced Apple Macaroons 52
  Strawberry Macaroons 48
  Summer Berry Macaroons 68
  Tangy Orange Macaroons 50

ginger: Chocolate Ginger
  Macaroons 32
Green Tea Macaroons 36
ground almonds 11

Hazelnut Chocolate Macaroons 26

icing sugar 11

lavender sugar: Violet & Lavender
  Macaroons 42
lemon curd
  Lemon Macaroons 24
  Summer Berry Macaroons 68
lemons
  Green Tea Macaroons 36
  Lemon Macaroons 24
limes: Sesame & Lime Macaroons 38

macaroons
  basic ingredients 11
  equipment 10
  oven temperatures 7
  step-by-step method 8–9
  storing 7
  top tips 7
Mango & Passion Fruit
  Macaroons 56
Mini Macaroons 76
Mint Chocolate Macaroons 40
Mont Blanc Macaroons 70

nuts
  Hazelnut Chocolate Macaroons 26
  Nutty Banana & Toffee
    Macaroons 54

Peanut Butter & Jam
  Macaroons 34
Pistachio Macaroons 20

oranges
  Christmas Macaroons 72
  Tangy Orange Macaroons 50

passion fruit: Mango & Passion Fruit
  Macaroons 56
Peanut Butter & Jam Macaroons 34
pineapple: Coconut & Pineapple
  Macaroons 62
piping macaroons 7, 10
Pistachio Macaroons 20

raspberries: Summer Berry
  Macaroons 68
raspberry jam
  Peanut Butter & Jam
    Macaroons 34
  Raspberry Ripple Macaroons 60
Rosewater Macaroons 18
Rum Truffle Macaroons 74

Saffron & Cardamom Macaroons 30
Sesame & Lime Macaroons 38
soft cheese
  Blueberry Cheesecake
    Macaroons 58
  Coffee Cream Macaroons 22
  Lemon Macaroons 24
  Sesame & Lime Macaroons 38
  Tiramisù Macaroons 44
  Violet & Lavender Macaroons 42
soured cream: Blueberry Cheesecake
  Macaroons 58
spices
  Christmas Macaroons 72
  Spiced Apple Macaroons 52
strawberries
  Strawberry Macaroons 48
  Summer Berry Macaroons 68
Summer Berry Macaroons 68
Sweetheart Macaroons 65

Tangy Orange Macaroons 50
Tiramisù Macaroons 44

Vanilla Macaroons 14
Violet & Lavender Macaroons 42